Openings 39
The Poetry Society of the Open University

Annual Anthology

of

OU Poets

2022

Copyright remains with the individual poets.
All rights reserved.

Published 2022 by Open University Poets.

ISBN 978-1-7399361-1-2

Editor: Sue Spiers
Cover: Dandelion Clocks by Ingrid Hill www.ingridhillart.co.uk

Printed by Lulu.com

Introduction

OU Poets is the Poetry Society of the Open University. It is open to any student or staff member, past or present. At the time of going to press there are about 90 members from all over the U.K. with some in mainland Europe and worldwide.

Members of the society submit poems to a magazine, which is produced 5 times a year, each one having a different voluntary editor. The magazine is not a publication *per se* and is strictly produced by the members for the members. There is a section for comment and criticism of members' work.

At the end of the year, members are asked to vote for the 20 poems they most appreciated from the 5 magazines produced that year. Those with the most votes, allowing for no more than one poem per poet, appear in the following year's issue of Openings. The anthology is as broad-based as the society itself and reflects the varied backgrounds, interests and tastes of the members.

If you would like more information about OU Poets, please contact the Secretary:
    Kimberley Pulling
    secretary@oupoets.org.uk

or the Chair:
    Polly Stretton
    chair@oupoets.org.uk
    Tel: (+44) 1886 830054 for postal address information.

Or visit our website at http://www.oupoets.org.uk

 @OUPoets

Contents

Poem	Name	Page
Not Hugging (Nor Drowning)	Alice Harrison	6
The Fixer	Nigel Kent	8
A Vile Affront	Denis Ahern	9
Katrina on Her First Hot Day	Jim Lindop	10
Vigil	Kimberley Pulling	12
Ghost Ship	Polly Stretton	14
A Brush with Reality	Rob Lowe	16
Call Me	Hilary Mellon	17
To Kiss Her	Phil Craddock	18
Glasses	Colin Rennie	23
Deep in my Heart	Christine Frederick	24
Judgement Day	Julie Anne Gilligan	25
Contemplating the Norm of Daily Terror	Cate Cody	26
Listerine	Judi Moore	27
A Long Stretch	Vicki Morley	28
Pick the Right Womb	David Dennis	29
Ophelia	Jane Avery	30
Green Rooting	Kate Young	32

Contents

Poem	Name	Page
Stress	Julie Stamp	34
Jabberwocky	Lem Ibbotson	35
Blow the Clocks Away	Karen Macfarlane	36
My Father at his Lathe	Barbara Cumbers	38
True Colours	Sally James	39
Old Battersea Bridge	K. J. Barrett	40
Lines in the Land	Ross McGivern	41
Walking on the Beach	Adrian Green	46
Secure in the Constant	Pru Bankes Price	47
Ode to an Octopus	Susan Jarvis Bryant	48
The Oak Keeps its Own Counsel	Sue Spiers	50
Nostalgia	Katherine Rawlings	51
Visualisation	Jenny Hamlett	52
View from the Cenotaph	Tim Field	54
The Exploratory Maiden	John Starbuck	55
A Thousand Suns, A Thousand Cranes	Rosie Douglas	56
The Morgan	Dave Sinclair	58
Acknowledgements		61

Alice Harrison

Not Hugging (Nor Drowning)

When I was knee high to the coal man's horse

I don't remember any hugging
nor even very much kissing.
My family's forte was waving
with a repertoire ranging
from wiggling fingers
through flapping wrists
to huge side-to-side arm gestures.
Visitors to our house would see
someone at our window
waving a greeting or farewell
for as long as they were in sight.
Even indoors, coming or going
we'd wave at each other.

By the time the coal man had upgraded to a lorry

I'd leave home occasionally.
A family member would come
to the station to see me off.
Once aboard the train
I'd lower the window
for some desultory talk
until relief arrived with a flag
and a whistle. My escort would jog
(waving) alongside the train until it
outpaced him or the platform ended.
One last wave at the waving dot
and I'd sink into my seat.

But that wouldn't be the end.
Along the route a best friend
waited to wave from a bridge
and a little further on, an aunt,
baby on hip, waved from her back step.
Only then, with a sigh, could I settle,
ready for the waiting world.

After he'd delivered we'd wave goodbye to the coal man.

Nigel Kent

The Fixer

When your teddy frayed from too much love,
I turned surgeon, nipping and tucking
until he looked and felt as good as new.

When I found you lost in mathematics' maze,
I turned guide, leading you through
the labyrinth of equations.

When you drifted in a sea of student debt
I turned receiver, salvaging the wreckage
and setting you on course to solvency.

When you crashed before your promotion panel
I turned restorer, filling, smoothing, polishing
until you shone again.

When you said you'd found the One,
I turned cheerleader, clapping from the side-lines,
singing encouragement,

but when he dropped you one year later
and you brought home the pieces of your heart to fix,
I could do nothing but fold my arms around you

and hold you tight.

Denis Ahern

A Vile Affront

Every hungry child is a vile affront
To justice demanding mercy unstrained.
To Rees-Mogg it's a political stunt

When the weakest are left to bear the brunt
As want and hardship spread uncontained
Every hungry child is a vile affront.

Help's at hand, Unicef at the forefront,
With food that these waifs might be sustained.
To Rees-Mogg that's a political stunt,

An unwelcome prod to a conscience blunt,
A barb to privilege greedily retained.
Every hungry child is a vile affront.

Compassion's met with a disdainful grunt
From the market motivated, spreadsheet brained,
And to Rees-Mogg, a political stunt.

Is seeking decency a fruitless hunt,
Where privilege unearned is thought ordained?
Every hungry child is a vile affront,
Yet to Rees-Mogg, a political stunt.

Jim Lindop

Katrina on her First Hot Day

She spellbinds me
(and her not three
....yet!)
with her whirligig of zest
and guileless sortilege…

Ah, yes!
She jangles giggles,
coaxing also me
to be not three
....yet.

She jiggles by me,
newly sun-free,
she bustles and
she busy-bees,
all hurly-burly
joie de vivre
on this dog day
....and me
within myself…not free,
light years away…She roundelays
and sashays her own
samba sun-dance –
....little one,
pinkening;

and me reviving dry
aspiring plants…
and rows to hoe…
and grass to mow…
    vital things…

She rounds me,
snares me,
bobby-dazzles me,
and her…(and me!)
not three
    yet.

Kimberley Pulling

Vigil

The final word. The final look.
I know they were, now.
How will I know the final breath
when there might yet be another?

When does this liquid life set hard?
Here/Gone.　　　　　Present/Past.
There must be one defining instant,
one moment.　　　　*Woman/Body*.

The slightest quiver. Pain, or plea?
Regret? Reproach? Was that the last
of You? A final grasp at life?
Or just a twitch. The last twitch.

Passion, person, presence, *Woman* –
such being couldn't end without
a sound, a sign, a *something* –
how will I know that moment?

Not the last beat, last breath, the noted time,
the shoulder-touch *She's gone*.
Present. Past. But somewhere between,
the moment.　　　　　Slower now

shallow　　and yet　　and also　　deeper.
Somewhere, teacups.　　Wait, did I miss –?
No, there's another.　　Was that it?
No, there's another.　　Was that it?

I will not know the last breath
but by the absence that follows.

I will not know the moment
but I will have been here.

Polly Stretton

Ghost Ship | A Sestina

Hope found *The Jenny*, the crew frozen dead,
the captain deceased at his log. He scribed
in pen and black ink, the written note said,
No food for seventy-one days, and he died.
But how, why, when, what was the watershed?
A cryptic chiller; all were mystified.

The ghost ship appeared, they were mystified,
it drifted through spooky mist, sound was dead,
weird shapes, foul smells, a scary watershed.
The final thing the captain did: he scribed,
wrote in his log, and then the poor man died.
The crew gone, my time has come, he said.

Ghost ships are abandoned, it's often said,
looming in the bay, sailors mystified,
as to how, why, when and where the men died.
Strange for all aboard to be stone cold dead.
The skipper out-lived them and he had scribed
through the crisis: the unknown watershed.

Ghostly trauma, a mystery watershed.
This was what fishermen on the shore said,
they crossed themselves and muttered, some scribed
like the captain; sea mist left them mystified.
All dead, they cried, their skin crawled, *All are dead*.
They couldn't imagine how they had died.

The mist swirled, the men glanced, shook, *All died*,
shuddered at the thought of the watershed,
was the ship ice-trapped, did that freeze them dead?
If so, how did captain live on? they said.
Sea mist rose, fell, and heard them mystified,
pondering most why the captain had scribed.

They had no logs, no words to be scribed,
they scratched their heads, why had the captain died?
They found no answer, remained mystified;
hearts laboured dread about the watershed,
There's more in heaven and earth… was often said,
One thing's for sure, they are all dead as dead.

No one found out how, why and where they died,
There's no answer, 'tis a ghost ship, they said,
and shaking their heads, remained mystified.

The Jenny was found frozen inside of an ice-barrier of the Drake Passage in 1840, almost 20 years after it first disappeared in 1823. https://www.astonishing legends.com

Rob Lowe

A Brush with Reality

Reality is looking old

You try to clean it up
But the bristles get worn out.

The dust returns and you grow cold
Despite the thermal springs of time.

Soon you will join the dust you swept;
Your years worn down to the bone

Reality is not made up.

Hilary Mellon

Call Me

call me
she said
though not out loud

those words
were screaming
only in her head

oblivious
he turned
he left the crowd

but ached
to yell his need
for her – instead

call me
he whispered – and
his head was bowed

call me
he said
he said

Phil Craddock

To Kiss Her

We met because of circumstance
At work. A random throw of chance
My job at times required that I assist her.
But from the day our pathways crossed
My heart was set, my head was lost
From then on all I wanted was to kiss her.

Bedazzled by her bright allure
I'd find excuse to talk to her
Emboldened by my ardour to impress her
And greeting me so smilingly
Completely unbeguilingly
She fed my flame of fantasy to kiss her.

We'd chat about the world's affairs
I got to know her likes and cares
On days when she was absent, how I missed her.
To hear her voice, to see her face
So full of playfulness and grace
No day passed by without a wish to kiss her.

But though imagination thrilled
And each encounter felt fulfilled
And though I'd no intention to resist her
I knew I had to wake up wise
If ever hope to realise
My dream of what it would be like to kiss her.

And so one day, dispelling doubt
I took a breath and asked her out
Though put in such a way as not to press her.
And when she said in swift reply
Why, yes of course! I wondered why
I'd feared I'd never find the chance to kiss her.

I let her choose the time we'd meet
And what we'd do and where we'd eat
Concerned that my involvement might distress her.
But when, again to my delight
She picked my place to end the night
My path was paved out perfectly to kiss her.

The evening flowed like sparkling wine
I drank her words, she laughed at mine
I found my every quip and comment pleased her.
And she was such good company
Intent, in turn, on pleasing me
What better reason could there be to kiss her?

We chatted on and on, attuned
To just ourselves, engrossed, cocooned
My foremost thought was not to second-guess her.
We talked of books and films admired
And travels planned and... things desired
I bit my tongue! Oh, how I longed to kiss her.

But conversation so sublime
Turned devil – we lost track of time
I had no plan of action to dismiss her.
So when she suddenly rose to go
The moment came – I moved – too slow!
She waved *Goodnight!* and left. I failed to kiss her.

Transfixed, struck still, behind the door
Just staring blankly at the floor
The spot where I'd felt destined to possess her
I wondered how I'd dashed the chance
So well laid out by providence
Just how had I so killed my call to kiss her?

The days that followed don't exist
They sank within a shameful mist
I know I lost the courage to address her.
But, strange to me, she carried on
Throughout my gloom her greetings shone
She'd seen no fool aspire and fail to kiss her.

And so she found me now and then
And put us back on track again
And for this faith of friendship how I blessed her.
And as our daily trysts resumed
I found myself once more consumed
With dreams to hold her close to me to kiss her.

But though we spent more evenings out
And still found all to talk about
And though she clearly liked me none the lesser
However well I had rehearsed
Each date progressed just like the first
I always somehow missed the chance to kiss her.

Now, cue the cod psychologist
Who'd hear my story and insist
That I'd become some sort of self-repressor:
Afraid I'd bring about an end
I'd settled for the role of friend
Not so – I burned with furnace fire to kiss her!

Her perfume, like a Siren lure
Her eyes, a universal cure
Her breezy tresses, dresses that caressed her.
The way she'd query what I said
Her mouth, her lips of ruby red
They all combined to make me ache to kiss her.

The truth, a much more mundane fact
And gathered far too late to act
And if she knew it – well, I couldn't quiz her:
I should have striven might and main
That night, to make my feelings plain
Not done, I'd lost all grounds on which to kiss her.

And if you'd asked me how I dealt
With knowing this, and how I felt
Compelled to treat her only as a sister?
Companion-wise I had no want
I was her friend and confidante
The only problem was – I craved to kiss her.

Immobilised like Tantalus
Unable to explain, discuss
Or venture any move which might oppress her
I lived to merely watch her lips
And envy her relationships
And turn away when others turned to kiss her.

Until, in time, our lives moved on
A brief farewell and she was gone
And I believed I'd really, deeply miss her.
But all the feeling I could find
If ever she was brought to mind
Was just a stupid, dumb desire to kiss her.

Colin Rennie

Glasses

The first time I wore my glasses in front of you
I felt more embarrassed than
The first time I was naked in front of you.
Now I wear my glasses most of the time
And occasionally go naked
But I never, as far as I'm aware,
Wear glasses when I'm naked.

Christine Frederick

Deep in my Heart

The stress and the pain, the anger, the woe,
The anguish, the sorrow, so rarely on show,
So well held together, so strong from the start,
I keep all these things that wound deep in my heart.

The hurt and the slights, the comments, which jar,
The problems, rebukes, those looks from afar,
The tears I hold back, the words that don't start,
I keep all these things that wound deep in my heart.

The work offered freely, dismissed with distain,
The experience of hands, giving nothing but pain,
The injustice, indifference and treatment, which charts,
I keep all these things that wound deep in my heart.

Julie Anne Gilligan

Judgement Day
The evil that men do lives after them
  – William Shakespeare

You oozed charm like a snail trail,
your faith in yourself solid as coprolite
and just as flexible, being of a similar origin.

Your passion was as overheated as permafrost.
You never knew the word 'cost',
never giver, always taker.

You plied persuasion like neat vodka.
Your smile leered from angelic to demonic:
do you know which you were?

If I met you now, I could happily cut you up
into minute slices of bad prose
but all you are worth is a few lousy metaphors.

Forgive and forget? Not in a thousand years
unless I shred all these remnant mites of disgust;
bury them deep in the dung heap of experience.

*Any resemblance to any person living, dead
or undead is purely intentional.*

Cate Cody

Contemplating the Norm of Daily Terror

Each time
when it's dark
and I reach the top of the park,
I am relieved

And then more than peeved
that this is even
a thing

Judi Moore

Listerine

There's a day or two's mouthwash left
in the bottle, which has gone a funny colour
'cos I leave it on the bathroom's sunny windowsill.

You'd have thrown it out ages ago,
started a new one, same as you did with me
not telling the old Listerine she was going in the bin.
Until that afternoon when you rushed home,
whipped out a roll of black plastic sacks
stuffed your life into them and lit out for
somewhere in Barnet. 'Staying with a friend.'
you said, 'Been offered a job.' Bullshit.

I sat there stunned, after you'd gone. Even then
I didn't cotton on for days. Until post came for you
and you'd left no forwarding address – I phoned you,
all concern: 'I've set all that up with the Post Office.'
you said, 'I didn't want to bother you.'
                That's when I suppose I really knew.

The following week I pulled out the sofa to hoover,
(Performing some strange sort of cleansing ritual)
and found, stashed behind it, your clanking collection
of empty vodka bottles. It was the final slap to realise
that what I tasted on your breath each morning
as you kissed me goodbye on your way out to work
wasn't Listerine – just a little something
to get you through the morning.

Vicki Morley

A Long Stretch

Mute swans stretch their long necks in flight
beaks arrowed towards lake water.
Sound of feathery wings.

We are all gathering ripe elder berries,
I look above and trip into a ditch.
Snap. Sound of cursing.

Armchair plump with cushions, velvet
throw, faded to maroon, books near.
Sound of yawning.

In the warm darkness of a boiler room
demi-johns are alive with wild yeast.
Sound of bubbles.

Bottles filled, a clinking, rattling, corking
storing time. My cast itches.
Sound of scratching.

A glass or two of last year's elderberry wine
glows with ruby fire, helps with healing.
Sound of sipping.

At Montol, no dancing for me, cast cut off.
One leg tanned, the other pale white skin.
Sound of bath filling.

David Dennis

Pick the Right Womb

The barn owl moves from left to right
not in a barn but in the field edged by woods
and the people dying in Syria don't know
anything about it – they don't say, I wish
I was in that field.
So, the barn owl is on the planet and the people
who are dying are on it, too.
The barn owl comes from an egg and we do too, sort of.
But it's the womb that matters. You've got to
pick the right womb to be happy.
Pick a womb in Guildford with a mother attached
who's Head of Art History at some university
and whose husband is not a killer
but is gentle, kind and drives a Lexus.
If you are born out of the wrong womb
you only have yourself to blame.
So, shape up, look out of the vaginal lips and
if what you see is chlorine green haze and barrel bombs –
go back up and try again.

Jane Avery

Ophelia
After John Everett Millais

you think I'm real
see poppies pansies
parted lips
a splintered bough
me
powerless

adjust your specs
escaping is a choice
you see I opted out
no not to die
abscond perhaps
where lover father brother lie
so deep the worms refuse to dine
in point
I'm choosing
not to be

I'm juxtaposed
erotic pure
my colours tell some kind of truth
the weeping willow
nettle
rose
this purple ring around my neck
bruises   no
just violets

saint or sinner
sound insane
eyes wide open
lips apart
I'll sink or swim inside your head
drown childish thoughts of innocence
a heroine   no
lying here was more than just an
afterthought
a balance in mortality
as simple as
forget me nots

Kate Young

Green Rooting

My Grandmother told me

she hailed from the Emerald Isle,
that her eyes of jade were made
from the jewelled tail of a mermaid,

that she bought her brogues
from a leprechaun,
the first of three wishes wasted,

that a cross scored
on a soda loaf crust
would silence the voice of the devil,

that a shamrock brings luck
if gathered at night, grass to palm
beneath the glint of the moon's eye,

that she kept these tales safely
tucked in a pocket of apple green
to preserve the taste of sweetness.

My Grandmother did not tell me

how her unwed mother was bundled
over the rolling glades to Galway,
to Tuam, where her secret was born,

she never spoke of the green notes
stuffed into hands of the childless,
nor of her home on the South coast,

she did not tell of the unmarked graves
she did not visit, where babies lay
unnamed, shamed on lands of the fallen,

she did not speak of the women,
of lives hung out to dry within
the walls of a Magdalene laundry,

she left no key to unlock her past,
no clues to trace the roots of green
but sure, she could spin a good yarn.

Julie Stamp

Stress

Too many thoughts in my head · too much awake in my bed · heart beating fast in my chest · brain never calm or at rest · stomach churns lemons (it feels) · more cups of coffee than meals · rather stay silent than speak · can't get my words out complete · won't go outside, hate the crowds · cottonwool mouth, head-in-clouds · can't stay relaxed, agitated · life is just *so* complicated · tell myself things aren't too bad · feels like I am going mad · people might help me – I doubt it · better not tell them about it · must not confess, cross the line · tell them that everything's fine

Lem Ibbotson

Jaberwocky

Twas Covid, and the nursy girl
Stuck needles into aged arms
All mimsy was the surgery
Without its charms.

Beware the nursy girl old man
With needle full of vaccine fluid.
Beware the doctor man who looks just like a druid.
She stuck her needle in my arm,
I never even shouted, 'ouch.'
She said, 'now you'll be covid-safe – for that I vouch.'

'And did you have the Pfizer jab?
Come to me arms me beamish boy
Now you are safe and virus-free.'
He chortled in his joy.

Twas Covid, and the nursy girl
Stuck needles into aged arms
All mimsy was the surgery
Without its charms.

Karen Macfarlane

Blow the Clocks Away

We're coming to see you! Soon!
We'll have days to spend,
precious currency when we've lost so many,
a plague-year of days
all fallen through our fingers.

Hundreds of tides have come in
and gone out, unpaddled
unsplashed
just waves passing by.

Twelve new moons climbed the bedtime skies
with no stories told.
They were special moons, too

a harvest-moon, gold
as a gingernut
on a night spiced with honeysuckle

a Super-moon so huge,
so close, we could all have reached out,
our hands from the north
yours from the south
and tickled it.

There was even a blue moon
but we never once got to see you.

Now, the small moons of the dandelion clocks
light up the dusk in our garden
and yours. Leave them there a little longer.
We're coming to see you.
And together
we'll blow the clocks away.

Barbara Cumbers

My Father at his Lathe

He is making chessmen, replacing lost pieces
from a length of dowel clamped to the lathe's spindle.
He leans on the armrest to steady his hand,
bends forward and applies a precise chisel to the wood,
the template guiding him. His right foot works the treadle,
turning and turning the flywheel. His left foot,
firm and flat to the floor, anchors him. His eyes narrow
in concentration. An array of chisels lies to hand,
some tiny, some shaped, all sharp, all ordered.
Small shavings fall like chrysanthemum petals.

It was I who lost the pieces, playing something like chess
in the garden, the board on a tree stump in long grass,
tossed in the air by a careless movement, irretrievable.
I want to help him replace them, yet know I can only
watch from close by, still and quiet, absorbing
the magic as a chess piece emerges from dowel, its spin
steady and central. A bishop, already shaped, awaits
the cleft of its mitre. A pawn is appearing beside it.
My father pauses, checks the template, selects another chisel,
then stoops again to the care of excision. And all the while
the flywheel spins, humming its small song of aptitude.
This is my father. This is his skill.

Sally James

True Colours

She wore a melancholy grey when she was sad
she never chose the colour it chose her
kind of slipped out of the wardrobe into her fingers.
Occasionally, when she was happy,
she found herself wearing shocking pink
youthful carefree days embedded in the seams.
When she was young, she wore vibrant red
it tinged her cheeks with excitement
made her bleed with unconsummated love.
Middle age found her wearing mauve
a mourning colour of sad regrets
and missed opportunities.
Her favourite colour was green
she was told green was for healing
it soothed her, made her feel whole.
She never liked black, it avoided her too
occasionally, it engulfed her in grief
soaked up unshed tears.
When she was in her sixties
blue wrapped her in contentment
made her think of the sea and sky.
Now she is old she is wiser
chooses her own colours
has a rainbow around her heart.

K. J. Barrett

Old Battersea Bridge
Nocturne Blue and Gold – James McNeill Whistler

At the dead hour,
When a sleeve of ash falls from a lighted cigarette,
Insomniacs look out from bedroom windows.

Ghostly silhouettes
Hauling themselves out of river silt,
Stare into blue air
Waiting for something to begin.

A firework unexpected,
The eye of the painter
Leaking blue and gold.

Ross McGivern

Lines in the Land

I am the Lines,
carved East-West, raked feet-deep
coughing up broken clay pipe and Roman coin.
Tilled and turned, fetching roots,
churning bronze and limestone plinth.

I am the Sunken Ground.
Settlements buried, preserved in time.
A portfolio of Bronze huts,
Roundhead camps and Georgian splendour.
Builders shall build but I'll always reclaim.

I am the Matter
The Tulip handled in Spring,
The Carrot tugged from its bed.
The Heron on the wing, the Lamb on the bank,
The Eel in the trap snapping its lock.

I am the Drains
cast straight like a road.
Silted and still, narrow waterways carry
the weight of yesteryear's barges.
Still and silted, narrow waterways dredge
the weight of yesterday's drivers.

I am the Grey-scale Skies.
A monochrome negative
developed over time.
A darkroom of images ringed
like the bypass that leads us away.

I am the Broad Orison.
The perfect landscape third.
Brushed mustards and rape seed irritation.
Ely cathedral smudged on the plane,
dusted by the wind
sermonising to a haze of field mice.

I am the Grit and Grain
blown by the eternal headwind.
Pollen spikes caught on an eyelash,
scratching your throat,
coating the crooked willow tree
bent and twisted by the broken stile.

I am The Paths
trodden by souls seeking prayer and prey.
I collect tithes from those who walk upon me,
exhibit anatomy from those unwilling to pay,
my trophies include lepers' limbs
and the offered knees
of Warriors, Saints and Martyrs.

I am the Flatness
the straight line on the screen
the lost pulse – the heartbeat harvested
from furrow and ridge.
Beep
        Bleat
                Bleep.
                        Gone.

But weep no more.

I am the Sound
of the cavernous empty hall
the village amphitheatre with crumbling walls.
A blank tape with which to record
the whispers of the wind,
the scream of the storm,
the shifts in silence heard
between hedgerow and turbine.

I be the Langwidge
yew carnt compoot,
the broight, woight, loight
of comoiynes out yesdee un
the coot ol' bouy wiv buckin' tongue
hoo amooz-es me wiv is foo vooz
or lil' ol' Duckie
hoos song be loike moos-ic to me eres.

I am the Past.
Drains dug by the Dutch.
Immigrants who shovelled shit,
heaved land to give us home.
Only to be mauled
by Fen Tigers roaming the nigh,
by Fen Tigers burning bright
lit by Jack o'Lanterns patrolling the Wash.

I am a Golden Treasury,
a pocket of cultural wealth.
I covet John's gold interred in marsh,
stole Clare's mind through rambling madness
and freed slaves in Clarkson's shadow.
Though you've forgotten, my memory is long.

I am the Anger
The impotent rage, the hatred, the fear,
the contempt for you all.
Possessed and Dispossessed,
Progressive and Regressive.
The Migrant, The Farmer, and Lodge Nominee.
Laboured and Labourer, Gangmaster and slave.
Reasoned and Rational, to the ones with books
and the ones who moved away:
you'll learn your place and you'll learn it good.

I am the Fen
and you are me.
You'll feel my shawl draped over cold shoulders.
You'll hear me wrestle with castled Rooks
who squat high in Oak to impose
their blackness upon you.

I am the Peat,
I am the Flood,
I am the Solitude,
I am the Fen,

I am on your tongue shaping your words,
in your guts twitching your vowels,
moulding your hands,
forcing your eyes to see the breadth of lines.
No matter how hard you scrub,
I'm here, always under your nails.

Adrian Green

Walking on the Beach

Walking on the beach
there is a moment
when the tide is not ready
to start its ebb

and the world beyond
that space between me
and the water's reach
has ceased to exist.

That moment between
the promise of then
and the mystery to come
stretches to infinity

and is gone
when the water recedes.

Pru Bankes Price

Secure in the Constant

sea and sky coalesce
       in infinite dark
              slow   slow

            a thread of light manifests
                a horizon whose
                      pale glow deepens
                            reflects stippled silver
                            across ocean's rough stretch

                                    yielding to day

Susan Jarvis Bryant

Ode to an Octopus

Shape-shifter of the sea, I've come to love
Your strange sophistication; out of place
In liquid labyrinths – your form sings of
Odd creatures from the sphere of outer space.
Yet here among anemones and fish,
An ocean star shines beautiful and bright.
Your flirty skirt of legs skims past a reef
In colours conjured by an inner wish
To hide your blushing pulse of pure delight,
As awestruck eyes look on in disbelief.

Houdini of the blue, you shrink and slink
Through crevices defying common sense.
Contortion and a dirty squirt of ink
Hoodwink eel and shark. Your skill's immense!
From jiggle-jelly soft to craggy rock,
You morph from smooth to rough with ease and speed,
Invisible to those who crave your taste.
The predators, they circle, and they flock;
Your flesh so sweet, they're driven by their greed –
A frenzied greed your guise will lay to waste.

Some see you as a gorgon of the waves;
A devil of earth's salty, surging swell,
A digger of dead sailor's briny graves,
A slimy siren crooning men to hell,
A Kraken sucking rasping gasps of breath
From lungs that burn for draughts of quenching air.
Once I feared you. Now I understand.
I see a soul, defying threat of death
With triple-hearted grace and wicked flair,
Fair mollusc of the surf and golden sand.

Sue Spiers

The Oak Keeps its Own Counsel

Tell me coy acorn
why your poison deters all
save nutkins and pigs

Tell me pale catkin
when you know to bloom – pepper
the sky with pollen

Tell me useful leaf
how to transform sun to air –
fill gutters with gold

Tell me wily root
what delve and twist you must make
to quench your nature

Tell me mossy bark
where within your skin rings lie –
memories circle

Tell me learned trunk
who takes the burden of age –
holds it together

Katherine Rawlings

Nostalgia

As children we shelled peas
In the kitchen garden
Tasted their sweet
Fresh pop on our tongues
With the smell of lavender
Enveloping our senses
And the music of the bees' hum
Mauve and mauve
Lavender and buddleia
White butterflies fluttering
In the moist heat of the sun's light
The world butter bright

Jenny Hamlett

Visualisation
        - not yours, mine

Don't give me the white sails
of a perfect red boat
sailing on a bright blue sea.

Don't take me down
to a woodland glade. Please
don't dish up a robin on a holly leaf.

Let me tell you where it's good
for me. I will have been walking
all day, map hung from my neck

following a thin path
looking out for the miners' hush
which might show where the track begins.

I've struggled through bog
on Sleightholm Moor and sat
on God's bridge, listening

to the A66 simply for company.
I've found my way over Ravock Castle,
am climbing to Race Yate Rigg

and there's nothing,
but tall yellow grasses
stroking my thighs,

cold wind from the north
caressing my cheeks,
a single swaledale calling

for her lamb. I'm alone
in sight of the ridge
with the lapwings rising.

Tim Field

View from the Cenotaph

I see you each year on Armistice Day,
approaching with grim, serious faces,
in sober suits and thick coats of steel grey
then 'moonwalking' back to your places.
Now assured of assuaging the guilt,
your rings of blood are laid down at my feet;
red plastic flowers, refusing to wilt,
will stand up righteous in shrouds of cold sleet.

Year after year, it's the same crowd who come,
few knowing of barbed pain and blanched scars.
And when back dancing to life's beating drum,
walking by, on a bus, in a car,
sailing past without as much as a nod,
just assuming heaven has me with God.

John Starbuck

The Exploratory Maiden

Curious at finding out what you're going to be,
What you will be good at, what you were
Designed for, like ducklings discovering
The dive and search for plants, pondweed,
Or little things which wriggle so…

The wildebeest does not know it's a gnu
Too. Shedding afterbirth and struggling
Upright on those leg things,
Chasing after mother and her milk,
Running from the hyena packs…

Identity is the thing: the batsman who never
Faced you before, expectant, unknowing,
So, therefore, vulnerable to change
Within six balls. If you can do that
You sow the doubts, hesitancies

Marking the greats, the Deadlies,
The Warnies, the Bosies if you're good.
Spread the field but bring one in,
Trigger movements will be in vain,
And do not trouble the scorers.

Rosie Douglas

A Thousand Suns, A Thousand Cranes

cranes cross the bleached sky
black etchings on white paper
the plum trees blossom
elders play hanafuda
after a day stooped in fields

half a globe away
men in suits and uniforms
shuffle their papers
a decision has been made
it is nineteen forty-five

destroyer of worlds
brighter than a thousand suns
humanity burns
women's shadows stain the walls
a city is vaporised

ten summers later
little Sadako stumbles
her legs distended
purple as wisteria
that climbs their wooden cottage

mother finds pebbles
to offer on the god-shelf
Amaterasu,
please save my failing daughter
the doctors shake their wise heads

there is a legend
that making one thousand cranes
will restore good health
Sadako sees a small hope
gathering the paper she folds

one hundred birds now
seven eight nine hundred done
urgently seeking
odd scraps for origami
until her hands work no more

still cranes fly outstretched
above the ume blossom
still men far away
designate children as
uncounted collateral damage

Dave Sinclair

The Morgan

Twas the night before Xmas and up on the roof
A sleigh was parked while its team soothed their hooves.
Santa was troubled and all in a dither
His reindeer were knackered and needed a breather.

So, Santa climbed down and looked in the shed.
He found an old Morgan, its battery quite dead.
A peek at the chassis revealed a bad crack.
One wheel had gone missing, its axle up on a jack.

Its chrome work was pitted, the frame had dry rot,
The kingpins were worn and the gear box was shot.
Both running boards scuffed, and the leather was torn,
And dull, faded paintwork made it look rather forlorn.

Just then, a trio rode up from out of the east,
They must have been summoned by the elves to assist,
They came bearing gifts, and were laden with tech,
Unleaded petrol, Castrol grease and GTX.

One tapped Santa's shoulder, and declared, *Have no fear,
I am Prince Lucas, and my friend's from Goodyear.*
The third and the tallest, said, *I'm Ed from far China,
Be prepared for our magic to save this old car.*

With a bang and a flash, the drive train was renewed,
The chassis re-welded, the ash frame re-glued.
A fresh coat of paint shone out bright in the star light,
New exhausts and twin horns gave the reindeer a fright.

The sleigh tumbled down from the roof to the drive
To be hitched up behind and the car came alive
The reindeer were turned out to graze on the lawn
Then Santa hopped in and with a wave he was gone.

So, tradition was preserved, and both near and far
The presents were delivered by a red Morgan car.

Poets

Name	Page	Name	Page
Denis Ahern	9	Nigel Kent	8
Jane Avery	30	Jim Lindop	10
Pru Bankes Price	47	Rob Lowe	16
K. J. Barrett	40	Karen Macfarlane	36
Cate Cody	26	Ross McGivern	41
Phil Craddock	18	Hilary Mellon	17
Barbara Cumbers	38	Judi Moore	27
David Dennis	29	Vicki Morley	28
Rosie Douglas	56	Kimberley Pulling	12
Tim Field	54	Katherine Rawlings	51
Christine Frederick	24	Colin Rennie	23
Julie Anne Gilligan	25	Dave Sinclair	58
Adrian Green	46	Sue Spiers	50
Jenny Hamlett	52	Julie Stamp	34
Alice Harrison	6	John Starbuck	55
Lem Ibbotson	35	Polly Stretton	14
Sally James	39	Kate Young	32
Susan Jarvis Bryant	48		

Acknowledgements

Adrian Green's 'Walking on the Beach' was editor's choice in April 2021 and appeared in *Littoral Magazine's* online edition September 2021

Jenny Hamlett's 'Visualisation' was first published in *Reach Poetry* issue 282 (Indigo Dreams)

www.ingramcontent.com/pod-product-compliance
Lightning Source LLC
Chambersburg PA
CBHW060219050426
42446CB00013B/3118